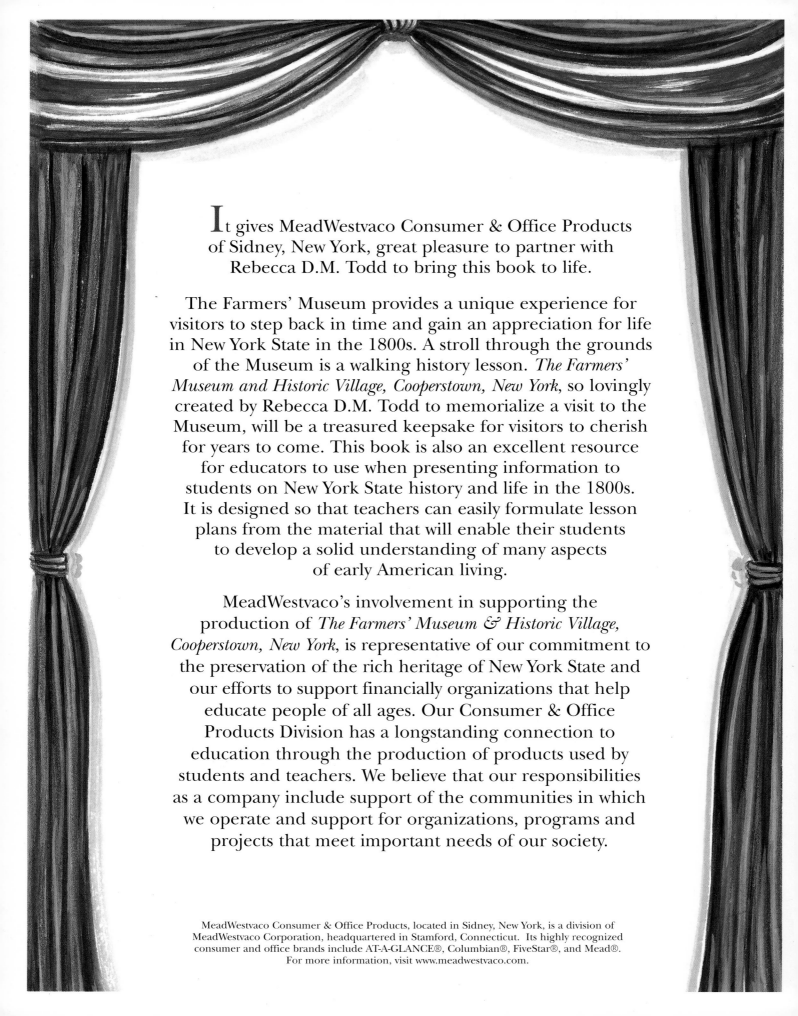

It gives MeadWestvaco Consumer & Office Products of Sidney, New York, great pleasure to partner with Rebecca D.M. Todd to bring this book to life.

The Farmers' Museum provides a unique experience for visitors to step back in time and gain an appreciation for life in New York State in the 1800s. A stroll through the grounds of the Museum is a walking history lesson. *The Farmers' Museum and Historic Village, Cooperstown, New York*, so lovingly created by Rebecca D.M. Todd to memorialize a visit to the Museum, will be a treasured keepsake for visitors to cherish for years to come. This book is also an excellent resource for educators to use when presenting information to students on New York State history and life in the 1800s. It is designed so that teachers can easily formulate lesson plans from the material that will enable their students to develop a solid understanding of many aspects of early American living.

MeadWestvaco's involvement in supporting the production of *The Farmers' Museum & Historic Village, Cooperstown, New York,* is representative of our commitment to the preservation of the rich heritage of New York State and our efforts to support financially organizations that help educate people of all ages. Our Consumer & Office Products Division has a longstanding connection to education through the production of products used by students and teachers. We believe that our responsibilities as a company include support of the communities in which we operate and support for organizations, programs and projects that meet important needs of our society.

MeadWestvaco Consumer & Office Products, located in Sidney, New York, is a division of MeadWestvaco Corporation, headquartered in Stamford, Connecticut. Its highly recognized consumer and office brands include AT-A-GLANCE®, Columbian®, FiveStar®, and Mead®. For more information, visit www.meadwestvaco.com.

The Farmers' Museum and Historic Village Cooperstown, New York

www.farmersmuseum.org

Publisher's Cataloging-in-Publication Data
(Prepared by The Donohue Group, Inc.)

Todd, Rebecca D. M. (Rebecca DeMulder Mietzelfeld)
The Farmers' Museum and historic village Cooperstown,
New York / written and illustrated by Rebecca D. M. Todd ;
in cooperation with The Farmers' Museum.

p. : ill. ; cm.
Includes bibliographical references.
ISBN: 0-917334-28-0

1. Farmers' Museum (Cooperstown, N.Y.)–Juvenile
literature. 2. Farm life–New York–History–19th century–Juvenile
literature. 3. City and town life–New York–History–19th century–
Juvenile literature. 4. New York (State)–Social life and customs–19th
century–Study and teaching. 5. New York (State)–History–19th
century–Study and teaching. I. Farmers' Museum (Cooperstown,
N.Y.) II. Title.

F129.C76 T63 2004
974.7/3

The
Farmers' Museum
and Historic Village

Cooperstown, New York

Written and illustrated by

Rebecca D. M. Todd

in cooperation with The Farmers' Museum

Deep in the heart of New York State . . .

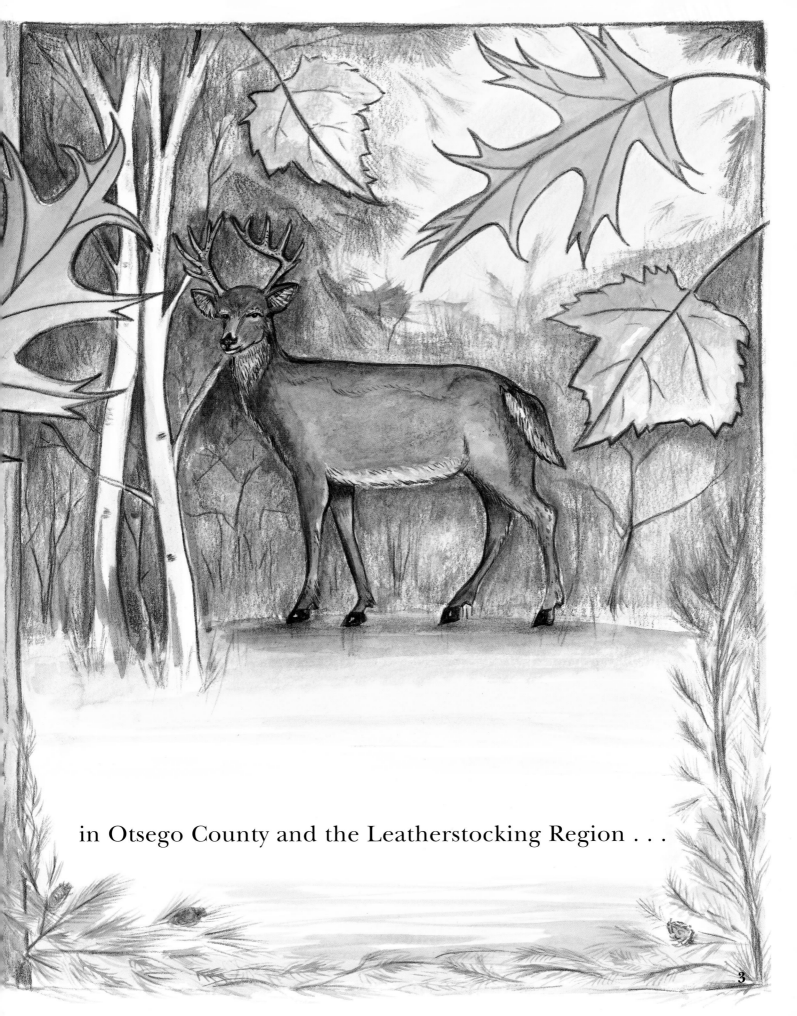

in Otsego County and the Leatherstocking Region . . .

at the headwaters of the Susquehanna River which

flows 444 miles southward across New York,

Pennsylvania and Maryland into the Chesapeake Bay

and the Atlantic Ocean . . .

Glimmerglass

on the shores of lovely

Lake Otsego, called Glimmerglass

for its shimmering, mirror-like beauty . . .

DOUBLEDAY FIELD

in the historic village of
Cooperstown, where tourists
crowd the streets in summer
visiting the world famous
National Baseball Hall of
Fame and Museum . . .

just up Lake Road,

nestled in the peaceful

countryside, is

The Farmers' Museum
and historic village!

Here busloads of curious school children

join visitors from far and wide on a journey back in time

to a New York State country village circa

(about the year)

1845.

11

The Farmers' Museum and historic village is a living history museum. The purpose of the museum is to educate people about the past.

The history of New York State agriculture (farming) is a very important part of the museum. Lippitt Farmstead is a complete working farm where the staff of the museum dress in historic clothing of the 1840s time period. They care for heritage breed farm animals and heirloom variety plants.

A hop yard is on the grounds of the museum. A hop yard is a farm field planted with hop vines. The flower of the hop plant is used to flavor

and preserve beer.

All around the open-air museum are historic buildings. The buildings have been moved to the museum and are restored as they would have appeared in the 1800s. Visitors entering these buildings can imagine themselves walking in the past.

There are displays about early homes, transportation, manufacturing, tools and trades. The blacksmith shop and printing office operate the same way they did in the early 1800s. Also on display is the Cardiff Giant, a huge stone man. He has been a silent, slumbering resident since 1948.

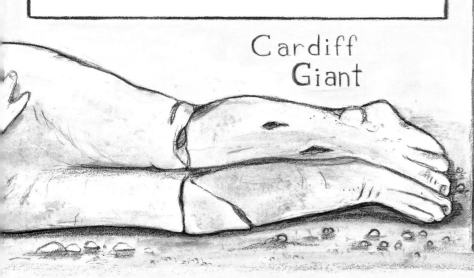

Cardiff Giant

When visitors walk the village streets the present day meets the long forgotten past, and there is much to learn. Visitors can sit at the old wooden desks in the Filer's Corners one-room school house and imagine children of different ages being taught together by one teacher. The teachers were called Masters for men and Mistresses for women and were nearly always very young people with little experience. At the top of the next page is a Reward of Merit from the 1800s. What do you think a Reward of Merit is? Below that are pages from an early text book called a primer. It is an elementary school book. How does your school day compare to that of the children in this Pictorial Primer?

LESSON VIII.

it	if	lo	ho
is	so	he	no
an	my	of	we
ax	ah	us	on

It is an ax.   Lo! it is he.
If it is so,   He is of us.
It is my ax.   Oh, no! is he?
Ah! so it is.   So we go on.

LESSON IX.

am	do	we	oh	on
as	it	go	fy	ye
to	so	at	up	no

I am as he is.   I am up on it.
Is he to do it?   He is up to it.
So we go at it.   I do as ye do.
Oh, fy! is it so?   No; do as we do.

LESSON X.

Is he, or am I, by it?
He is to go by me.
If it be so, do it.
As ye do, so do we.

LESSON XXIX.

boys	rides	with	hoops
girls	cart	their	swing
one	some	guns	jump
flies	ball	swords	rope
kite	train	roll	dolls

THE PLAY-GROUND.

See the boys and girls at play.
One boy flies his kite, and one
   rides in his cart.
Some play at ball; some train
   with their guns and swords.
The girls roll their hoops, or ride
   in the swing.
Some jump the rope, and some
   play with their dolls.

In the 1800s most Americans lived on farms. Every member of a farm family had to work very hard. Animals and people depended on the food grown on the farm to sustain them. At the museum, Lippitt Farmstead recreates this way of life. Pigs, ducks, chickens, turkeys, cows, oxen, sheep, such as the Southdown below, and a draft horse are raised. In 1845, livestock and poultry such as these would have provided a family with meat, eggs, wool, milk and sources of power for pulling farm equipment and transportation vehicles. The animals on Lippitt Farm are all heritage breeds. This means that they are the animal breeds that would have been found on a rural (country) New York State farm in 1845.

On a farm, women's work was never done. Country women cared for children, cooked over open hearth fireplaces, and raised kitchen herb and vegetable gardens. Here is a favorite recipe at Lippitt Farm House. It is common Cup Cake from an 1832 cookbook. This type of cake is also called "1,2,3,4" cake. Can you discover why?

"CUP CAKE:
Cup cake is about as good as pound cake and is cheaper.

One cup of butter
Two cups of sugar
Three cups of flour
Four eggs

Beat well together baked in pans or cups."

*Using a wooden spoon, cream soft butter and sugar, add lightly beaten eggs, then add flour slowly. Beat until thick. Bake at 350° for 35 min. in greased cup cake tins. YUM! * Ask an adult for help.*

Farm women spun their own wool and flax fibers by hand. The woman pictured below is using a hand-powered machine called a click reel or skein winder to measure lengths of yarn. The reel winds yarn and makes a loud clicking sound when it has wound 80 yards. (80 yards equals one knot of yarn.) Many farm houses had looms set up for weaving homespun yarns. Tablecloths, shawls, carpets, blankets and flannel fabric could all be woven on home looms.

Behind Lippitt Farm House is a kitchen garden with a high wooden fence surrounding it. The fence protects the plants from hungry rabbits, woodchucks and white-tailed deer. The wide variety of plants grown in the garden include potatoes, beans, beets, corn, melons, onions, parsnips, peas, radishes, pumpkins, cabbage, squash, tomatoes, turnips, rutabaga, lettuce, carrots, cucumbers, grapes and currants. In the 1840s, garden crops were not only valued as food, but also as a form of currency. (Money is a form of currency.) Farm crops were traded or bartered in the same way people today exchange money for goods and services.

Another important crop grown on some New York State farms in the nineteenth and early twentieth centuries was hops. Hops were a specialty cash crop. A large harvest of quality hops could be sold for a lot of money. This photo taken around 1880 shows hop pickers and field hands who earned cash for their work. In rural New York, more women picked hops than men. Why do you think women would have been important laborers (workers)? The hop flower looks like a small green pine cone. It grows in clusters like grapes, on long climbing vines which need to be supported. Look behind the workers to see the hops on poles.

In 1845, if farm families had cash to spend, they might take a trip to a store similar to Todd's General Store at the museum. If they didn't have cash, which was the case more often than not, they could still barter-trade farm produce, animal products, homemade goods or services for store merchandise. Local products, either purchased for cash or taken in by a storekeeper on trade, would have been for sale in the store or transported to sell in urban (city) markets. These could have included hog bristles, maple sugar, flax seed, pine boards and shingles, wheat, oats, corn, barley, potash, cheese, lard, butter, eggs, dried apples, knitted woolen stockings or mittens. Services such as plowing or hauling firewood were also bartered. Below are toys that may have been for sale in a store in 1845. Do you recognize these toys?

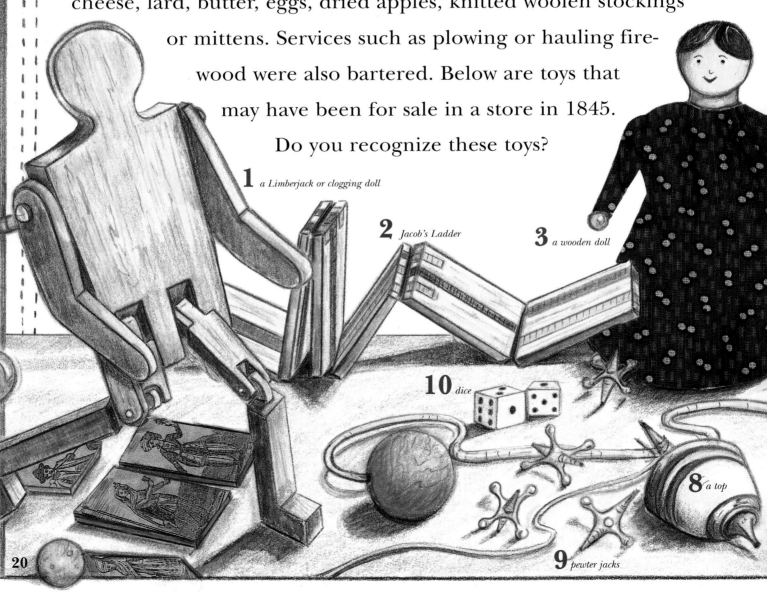

1 *a Limberjack or clogging doll*

2 *Jacob's Ladder*

3 *a wooden doll*

10 *dice*

8 *a top*

9 *pewter jacks*

Storekeepers also provided rural communities with a wide range of goods from around the country (domestic) and the world (imports). In the 1840s, imported and domestic merchandise, transported from urban centers like New York City and Albany, could be purchased in rural New York State. Just like today, store owners placed advertisements in newspapers to get people to come into their shops. The items below were taken from store ads placed in Cooperstown newspapers between the years 1840 and 1847. Can you still buy these things on a shopping trip today?

White & Brown Sugars	Toys of all descriptions	Violin Strings
Canton Teas	Whalebone (Baleen)	Sap Buckets
Pepper & Coffee Mills	Horn & Fancy Silk Buttons	Oils: Linseed & Whale
Oranges & Lemons	Bonnet Ribbons & Straw Hats	Playing Cards
Confectioneries & Chocolate	Indigo & Madder Dyes for cloth	Skates & Slates
Molasses, Flour & Raisins	Printed Calicoes (cotton cloth)	Buffalo Robes
Ginger & Cinnamon	Looking Glasses	Horse Blankets
Watercolors	Perfumery	Sheep Shears
Iron Washboards	Tyrian Dye for coloring hair, whiskers	Paper Hangings (wallpaper)
Pavilion Water from Saratoga Springs	Silk Parasols	Carriage Springs
Spanish Hoods for Children	(candle) Snuffers	(gun) Powder & Fish Hooks
London Sealing Wax	Rat & Mouse Traps	Axes & Hoes
Beaver Cloth	Suspenders	Dr. Z. W. Lay's Cough Pills

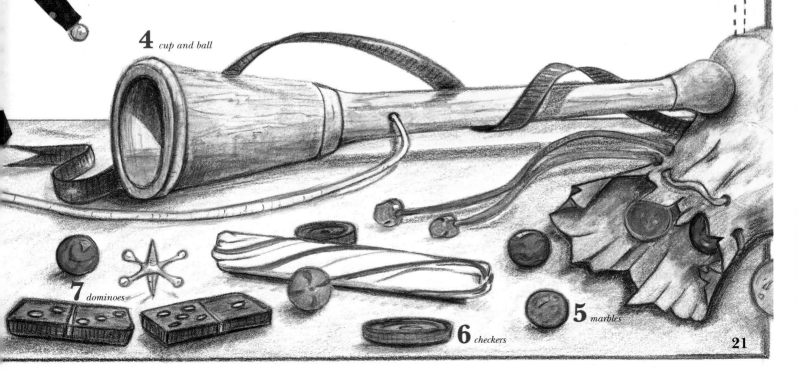

4 *cup and ball*

7 *dominoes*

6 *checkers*

5 *marbles*

In the museum's sunny garden, beside Dr. Thrall's Pharmacy, plants that are used to make medicines are grown. Many of these plants contain naturally occurring chemical compounds which are still found in drugs used by people today. Early healers really did have useful tonics, recipes and remedies to help their patients. Some of the plants that are found in the garden are: mint, chamomile, parsley, garlic, comfrey, bee balm, yarrow, cup plant, lavender, pot marigolds and dill.

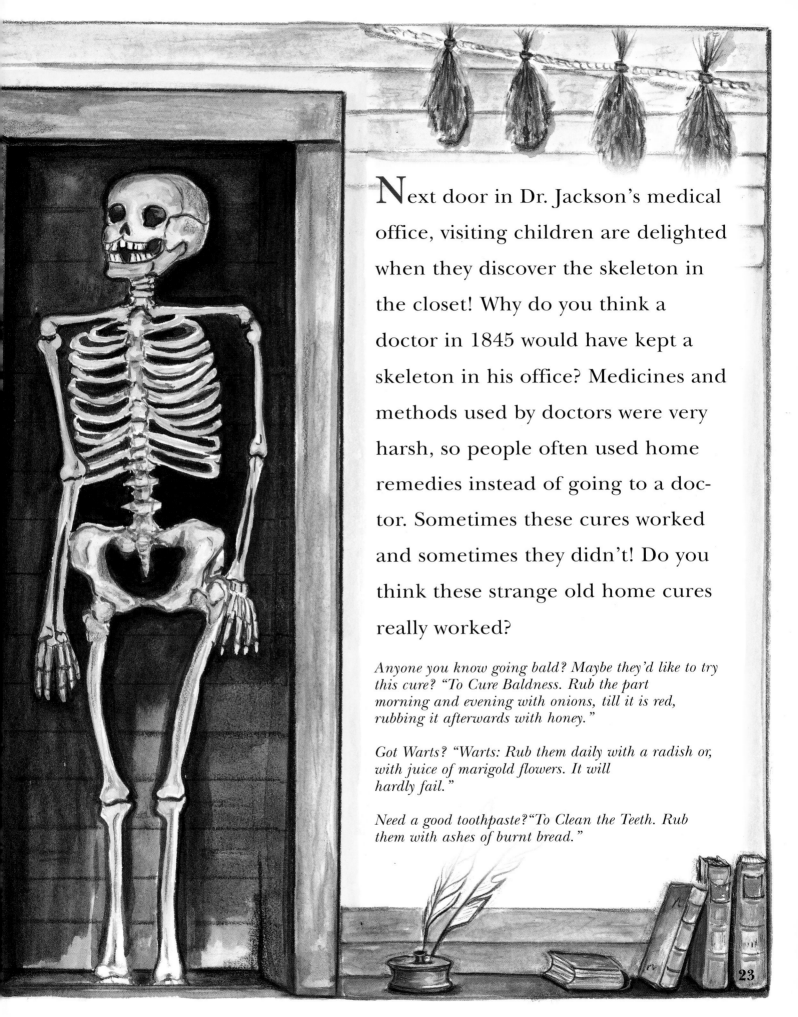

Next door in Dr. Jackson's medical office, visiting children are delighted when they discover the skeleton in the closet! Why do you think a doctor in 1845 would have kept a skeleton in his office? Medicines and methods used by doctors were very harsh, so people often used home remedies instead of going to a doctor. Sometimes these cures worked and sometimes they didn't! Do you think these strange old home cures really worked?

Anyone you know going bald? Maybe they'd like to try this cure? "To Cure Baldness. Rub the part morning and evening with onions, till it is red, rubbing it afterwards with honey."

Got Warts? "Warts: Rub them daily with a radish or, with juice of marigold flowers. It will hardly fail."

Need a good toothpaste? "To Clean the Teeth. Rub them with ashes of burnt bread."

In 1845, most of the inhabitants of rural New York State villages, those similar to the village recreated at the museum, were immigrants from Europe or their descendants.

It is also important to know that North American Indian civilizations thrived in the New York State region for thousands of years before the arrival of the Europeans. To this day, descendants of Native New York Indian civilizations, known today as the Algonquin and Iroquois, also referred to as Hau-de-no-sau-nee in the original Native language, make their homes within the New York State region. *Haudenosaunee,* commonly pronounced hoe-dee-no-SAW-nee, means "The People of the Long House."

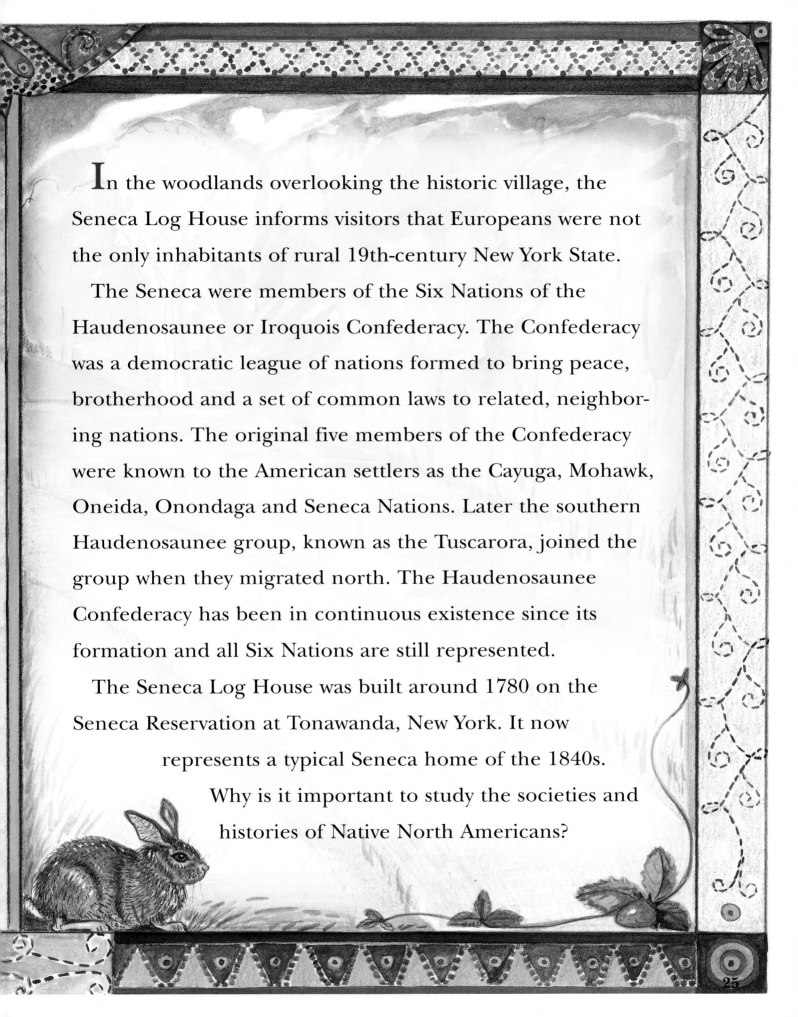

In the woodlands overlooking the historic village, the Seneca Log House informs visitors that Europeans were not the only inhabitants of rural 19th-century New York State.

The Seneca were members of the Six Nations of the Haudenosaunee or Iroquois Confederacy. The Confederacy was a democratic league of nations formed to bring peace, brotherhood and a set of common laws to related, neighboring nations. The original five members of the Confederacy were known to the American settlers as the Cayuga, Mohawk, Oneida, Onondaga and Seneca Nations. Later the southern Haudenosaunee group, known as the Tuscarora, joined the group when they migrated north. The Haudenosaunee Confederacy has been in continuous existence since its formation and all Six Nations are still represented.

The Seneca Log House was built around 1780 on the Seneca Reservation at Tonawanda, New York. It now represents a typical Seneca home of the 1840s.

Why is it important to study the societies and histories of Native North Americans?

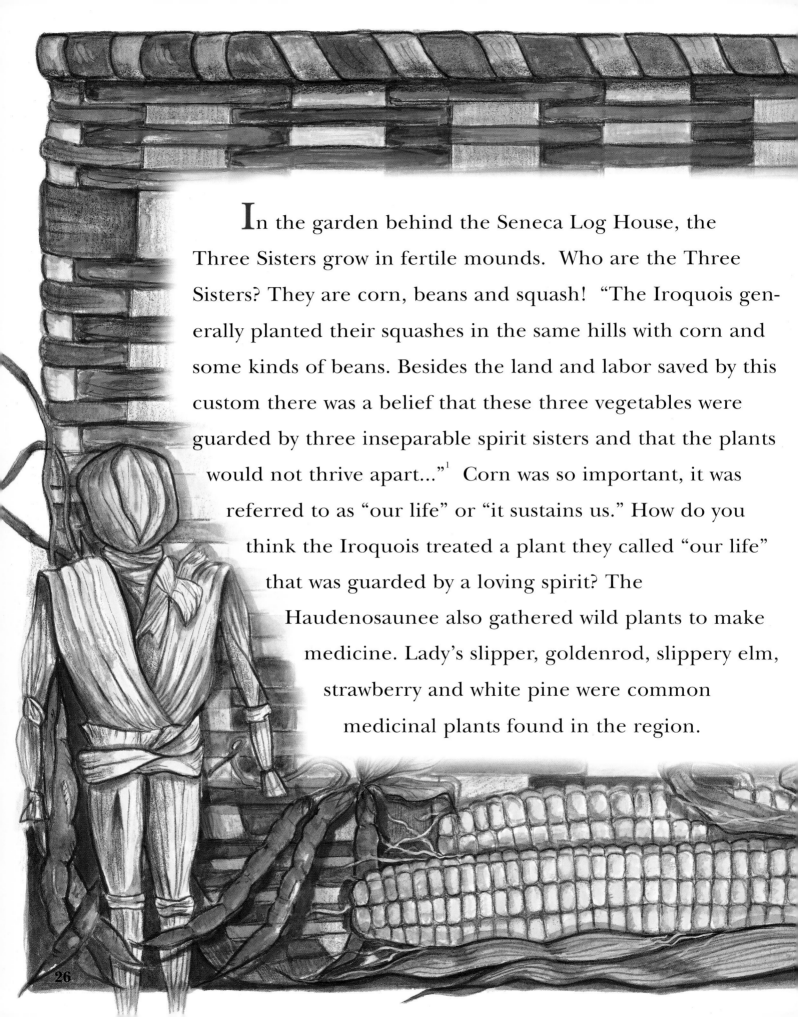

In the garden behind the Seneca Log House, the Three Sisters grow in fertile mounds. Who are the Three Sisters? They are corn, beans and squash! "The Iroquois generally planted their squashes in the same hills with corn and some kinds of beans. Besides the land and labor saved by this custom there was a belief that these three vegetables were guarded by three inseparable spirit sisters and that the plants would not thrive apart..."[1] Corn was so important, it was referred to as "our life" or "it sustains us." How do you think the Iroquois treated a plant they called "our life" that was guarded by a loving spirit? The Haudenosaunee also gathered wild plants to make medicine. Lady's slipper, goldenrod, slippery elm, strawberry and white pine were common medicinal plants found in the region.

By studying agricultural practices, historians learn how people lived in the past and many details about their cultures. Even today there are stories, myths and celebrations that honor the cycles of nature and the blessings of a bountiful harvest. Now that you have learned about the history of New York State farming, take a moment to think about the amazing assortment of fresh foods that modern farmers provide for us all year round. Who grew, harvested and transported these foods to market? Today people receive the gifts of the Great Mother Earth without a thought of where they came from. If we all gave back to our Mother Earth more than we took, no one would be hungry and all the world's people could live in harmony.

Thanks for joining this book tour!

For Your Information:

Cover: The girl from 1845 was designed by combining three elements: a circa 1845 painting entitled "Picking Flowers," attributed to Samuel Miller; a cut paper silhouette of a girl jumping rope, circa 1840, by August Amant Constance Fidele Edouart; and a swatch of authentic cloth.

Stenciling or "Fancy Painting": People in the 19th-century enjoyed decorative accents in their homes. Stenciling walls and floors was a popular way to add color and design to a room. The stencils used to create the yellow endpapers belonged to the collection of my grandmother, Mabel Frost Clinnick.

Heritage Breeds: The domestic farm animal breeds represented in this book are: Title page: Southdown sheep originating in England. Animals next to stone wall: Duroc pig originating in New York, Dominique chicken introduced to the United States by the French, Cheviot sheep originating in the Cheviot Hills of Scotland, Percheron horse originating in France. Folk Art bull: Durham oxen originating in Durham, England. (various sources listed)

Typeset: The type for "*The Farmers' Museum and Historic Village, Cooperstown, NY*" on the two title pages was set and printed by hand at the Otsego Herald office at The Farmers' Museum.

Penmanship: The painted word "Glimmerglass" and the author's name were designed using 19th-century penmanship samples.

Origin of Glimmerglass: James Fenimore Cooper (1789-1851) is considered America's first major novelist. In Cooper's 1841 romantic novel, *The Deerslayer,* the character Hurry Harry, referring to Lake Otsego states: "Among ourselves, we've got to calling the place the 'Glimmerglass,' seeing that its whole basin is so often fringed with pines, cast upward from its face; as if it would throw back the hills that hang over it." (from *The Deerslayer*, chap. II, count about six paragraphs backwards from the end of the chapter – consultant MacDougall/James Fenimore Cooper Society/*from 1st Ed., Vol. I, p.42)*[1]

Leatherstockings: These are leg guards made of leather, which extend from the ankle to the thigh and are held in place by a belt extending down from the waist. They protected the legs of men when they traveled through dense forests.

Historic Cooperstown: The brick and ironwork gateway, with the dog ready to play ball, is the entrance to Doubleday Field, which is famous in baseball lore.

"Indian Hunter": In the illustration of Lake Otsego, the North American Indian hunter is a depiction of a statue entitled, "*Indian Hunter,*" by American sculptor, John Quincy Adams Ward (1830-1910). The sculpture located in Lakefront Park in Cooperstown is an 1897 copy of an original located in New York City's Central Park which is signed "J. Q. A. Ward/Sculptor/N.Y. 1866." For this sculpture, Ward traveled from New York City to the Dakotas to make studies of North American Indians in pencil on paper and red wax (3-D models). (author Sharp, pp. 44-45, 165-166)

Folk Art: The illustration for the page with the tiny school buses was designed to look like a Folk Art painting. Folk artists are usually self taught and often work from memories. The style of this painting shows many things happening at one time from different directions and on many levels.

Circa: (pronounced like circus with a short "a" sound at the end) A term historians use to indicate an approximate date.

"1, 2, 3, 4" Cup Cake: To vary this basic recipe include the addition of a handful of currants, raisins or coconut.

The Cardiff Giant: A hoax (rhymes with oaks) is a deliberate attempt to fool people into believing that something which is false is actually true. The Cardiff Giant is a stone sculpture. The giant's 19th-century creators claimed that it was the remains of a petrified giant!

Hop Culture: According to author Michael A. Tomlan, in his 1992 book, *Tinged With Gold: Hop Culture in the United States,* "In the East, women performed much of the field labor in harvesting because most men could not leave their farms or factory jobs for the entire harvest season. In general, women and girls were believed to be better pickers, and they were willing to work for less … As one Otsego grower wrote at mid-century, 'I have often heard the remark, that our hops are all picked by females,' … Young children would be brought along, but they soon tired of any repetitive chores and were allowed to amuse themselves." (Tomlan, pp. 119-20)[2]

Potash: To create potash, which is the compound potassium carbonate, water is slowly poured over the ashes of burned wood. The liquid collected in this leaching process is then boiled down in large open kettles to obtain the white solid residue or ashes in the pot. Potash was used in the preparation of simple soap.

Historical Research: Want to know more about the terms on the store lists? Type these terms (one at a time) into an internet search engine and see what you can learn: history of ice skates - history of roller skates - wallpaper history - history of Saratoga Springs - history of parasols - madder dye - indigo dye - whale oil - buffalo robes - whalebone or baleen - beaver cloth - candle snuffers - hog bristles. (Do you think the skates on the store list are ice skates, roller skates or both? Why?)

Origin of the name Iroquois: According to author Evan T. Prichard in his 2002 book, *The Native New Yorkers: The Legacy of the Algonquin People of New York*, "the term *irinakoiw* of the Algonquin tribe of Canada … means 'they are real adders' or 'they are mean.'" The French may have mistaken this insulting term for the proper name of the *Haudenosaunee* (also spelled Hodenosuannee in Prichard's book). *Haudenosaunee*/Hodenosuannee is "The commonly accepted word for these people… although elders say Ongwe-Oweh is more correct." (Prichard, p. 29)[3] ("Ongweoweh" translates as "Original Men" from author Parker, Book 3, p. 9)[4] Another Haudenosaunee pronunciation is:"hoe–dee–no–SHOW–nee." (www.iroquois.net– Barbara A. Gray)

Haudenosaunee or Iroquois Artistry: The borders illustrating the Seneca Log House and Three Sisters pages were carefully designed by observing Seneca and *Haudenosaunee* or Iroquois bead and quill embroidery work and basketry in the Eugene and Clare Thaw Collection of North American Indian Art, at the Fenimore Art Museum, Cooperstown, New York.

Haudenosaunee or Iroquois Medicine: "Keeper of the Medicine" was the name given to the official collector of medicinal plants. It was believed that the "keeper" had a special relationship to the plant world and could communicate directly with plant spirits. Both women and men gathered plants for medical purposes. While gathering, they would make offerings to the plant spirits (usually sacred tobacco), then remind the plants of their duty to be of service and ask for their assistance in the work of healing humankind. (Various sources listed–specifically, but not exclusively, author Herrick & consultant Rickard)

Good-bye!

O: nen kiwahe!
(Mohawk for: *Until we meet again*)*

Special Thanks to Consultants and Friends

Dr. Gilbert T. Vincent, former President of the New York State Historical Association (NYSHA) and The Farmers' Museum (TFM)

Yvonne Cornell, former Secretary and **Maureen Dill**, Administrative Assistant to the President, NYSHA/TFM

Garet Livermore, Director of Education, NYSHA/TFM

Dave Rickard, former Native American Specialist, The Farmers' Museum

Mike Tarbell, Iroquois Indian Museum Educator, Mohawk – Turtle Clan

Hugh MacDougall, Cooperstown Village Historian/James Fenimore Cooper Society

Mary Grace Flaherty, Director, Sidney Memorial Public Library, An extra thank you for reference/editing assistance and all-around moral support!

MeadWestvaco Consumer and Office Products

Mrs. Lepik & Mrs. Rowe, Specialists in Fourth Graders!

Dr. Paul D'Ambrosio, Chief Curator, NYSHA/TFM

Joe Caffery, Farm Manager, The Farmers' Museum

Daniel Goodwin, Editor & the late **Carole Mihalko**, formerly Associate Editor of *NY History*

The Farmers' Museum Educators and Staff:
(*listed alphabetically*) **Garry Aney, Wayne Coursen, Sara Keegan, James Kelly, Mary Margaret Kuhn, Paul Kuhn, Patrick MacGregor, Gwen Miner, Jo Mish, Dorothy Rathbun, Ted Shuart, Marieanne Tafel, Greta Taylor, Betty Thompson, Ann Vickery, Wendy Weeks, Lillian Yerdon, and Pat Young**

The Marvelous Librarians at the **NYSHA Research Library**

The National Baseball Hall of Fame and Museum for authorizing the use of their name in this publication

Carol Waller, Cooperstown Mayor, for authorizing the use of Doubleday Field

M & M & R & S Consultants (My wonderful family!)

Madame Librarian Extraordinaire, **Janet Glantz** for inspiration

Farmer Brown and Daughter, Agricultural Consultants!

Patrick VerValin, Pharmacist, Pharmacology Consultant

Charles Collier, Technology/Science Teacher, Technology Consultant

* Source: Barbara A. Gray - www.iroquois.net

IN MEMORY OF MY BELOVED FATHER
Thomas Sebron DeMulder

Primary Sources:

Award of Merit: by Anon., [United States] (found in Oneonta, NY, n. d.) author's collection

Primer: *Sander's Pictorial Primer,* by Charles W. Sanders, (NY: Ivison, Blakeman, Taylor & Co., 1858) pp. 13 & 23. author's collection

Cup Cake Recipe: *The American Frugal Housewife.* Dedicated to those who are not ashamed of economy, by Mrs. Child (Lydia Maria Child), (Boston: Carter, Hendee, and Co., 1832) p. 71. rpt. 1985 by The Friends of the Libraries of the Ohio State University

Photo: *Hop Pickers/Field Hands,* by Anon., [United States] (found in Homer, NY, n. d.) author's collection

Buying & Selling Advertisements: *Freeman's Journal,* Cooperstown Newspaper, pub. on Saturday mornings by John H. Prentiss, (Cooperstown, NY: bound issues Sept. 5, 1846 - Aug. 21, 1847)

Advertisements cont.: *Otsego Republican,* Cooperstown Newspaper, ed. A. M. Barber; Isaac K. William & Co., Sept. 7, 1849; William L. Clark, Feb. 14, 1842, (Cooperstown, NY: bound issues Feb. 17, 1840 – May 9, 1842)

Folk Remedies: *Domestic Medicine or A treatise on the Prevention and Cure of Disease containing Eight Hundred Safe and Valuable Receipts,* by Rev. John Wesley, M. A., (Lowell: 1843) pp. 13, 61, 65.

Work Cited in Text:

1) Arthur C. Parker. *Iroquois Uses of Maize and Other Food Plants.* Ed. William Fenton, (Syracuse, NY: Syracuse University Press, 1968, Book 1) pp. 91-92.

Works Cited in "For Your Information":

1) James Fenimore Cooper. *The Deerslayer: or The First War-Path.* (Philadelphia, Lea & Blanchard, 1841, vol. I) p. 42.

2) Michael A. Tomlan. *Tinged with Gold: Hop Culture in the United States.* (Athens, GA & London: The University of Georgia Press, 1992) pp. 119-20.

3) Evan T. Pritchard. *Native New Yorker: The Legacy of the Algonquin People,.* (San Francisco & Tulsa: Council Oak Books, 2002) p. 29.

4) Arthur C. Parker. *The Constitutions of the Five Nations.* Ed. William Fenton, (Syracuse, NY: Syracuse University Press, 1968, Book 3) p. 9.

Selected List of Websites Consulted:

http://www.iroquois.net (viewed Jan. '04)
http://www.iroquoismuseum.org (viewed Jan. '04)
http://www.mohawknation.org (viewed Feb. '04)
http://www.peace4turtleisland.org (viewed Feb. '04)
http://www.sixnations.org (viewed Jan. '04)

Selected List of Works Consulted:

A System of Universal Geography, by William Channing Woodbridge, (Hartford, CT: Oliver D. Cook & Sons, 1824) A Source for Imports

"The Art of the Silhouette." AMERICANA, by Richard F. Snow, (New York, NY: The American Heritage Society, Nov. 1973, vol. 1, No. 5) Source for August Amant Constance Fidele Edouart Silhouette

The Country Store in Early New England, by Gerald Carson, (Sturbridge, MA: Old Sturbridge Village, 1955, rpt. 1963 & 64)

From Candy to Gunpowder: A Visit to the General Store in 1845, by Jo Mish, (Cooperstown, NY: New York State Historical Association, 1996)

Dating Fabrics: A Color Guide 1800 – 1960, by Eileen Jahnke Trestain, (American Quilter's Society: Paducah, KY, 1998)

Feeding the Body and Soul: Haudenosaunee Agriculture in the 19th Century, created by Janet Williammee and Dave Rickard, (The Farmers' Museum, Cooperstown, NY, 2002)

Heritage Breeds of Animals and [Heirloom Varieties of] Plants at The Farmers' Museum, by The Farmers' Museum: Study Guide, (Cooperstown, NY, 2001)

Heritage: The Magazine of the NYSHA, ed. By Paul S. D'Ambrosio, (Cooperstown, NY, NYSHA Spring and Winter 1993)

Indians of North America: The Eight Culture Areas and How Their Inhabitants Lived Before the Coming of Whites, by Paula A. Franklin, (New York: David McKay Company, Inc., 1979) A Source for Iroquois Confederacy or League

The Iroquois, by Barbara Graymont, Ph.D., (New York & Philadelphia: Chelsea House Publishers, 1988)

Iroquois Medical Botany, by James W. Herrick, (Syracuse University Press, 1995) A Source for Iroquois medical practices and plants

John Quincy Adams Ward: Dean of American Sculpture, by Lewis I. Sharp, (Newark: University of Delaware Press; London & Toronto: Associated University Press, 1985) Source for information on sculptor J. Q. A. Ward

Parker on the Iroquois: Iroquois Uses of Maize and Other Food Plants: The Code of Handsome Lake, the Seneca Prophet: The Constitutions of the Five Nations, by Arthur C. Parker, ed. William N. Fenton, (Syracuse, N Y: Syracuse University Press, 1968) Source for Iroquois Governance and Agriculture

Magic and Medicine of Plants: A Practical Guide to the Science, History, Folklore and Everyday Uses of Medicinal Plants, project director, Inge N. Dobelis, (Pleasantville, N Y, Montreal: The Reader's Digest Association, Inc. 6th printing, 1992) Source for medicinal plants native to North America

Rural Hours, by Susan Fenimore Cooper, ed. Rochelle Johnson and Daniel Petterson, (originally published: New York: G. P. Putnam: London: Putnam's American Agency, 1859) (rpt. Athens, GA & London: the University of Georgia Press, 1988) Source for educational practices, farm and "domestic manufactures"

The Botanic Family Physician or the Secret of Curing Diseases with Vegetable Proportions, by Dr. L. Sperry, (Cornwall, VT: published by the author, 1843)

The Joy of Spinning, by Marilyn Kluger, (New York: Simon & Schuster, 1971)

The Legend of the Lady Slipper, by Lise Lunge-Larsen & Margi Preus, (Boston: Houghton Mifflin Co., 1999) Children's legend about the medicinal properties of the lady slipper flower

The Old Country Store, by Gerald Carson, (New York: Oxford University Press, 1954)

The Oneota: Medicine in the Forest, by Willard E. Yager, (Oneonta, N Y: Oneonta Herald Pub. Co., 1911)

"The Poor Widow's Mittens." Rupert Cabell and Other Tales, by Joseph Alden, D. D., (New York: Gates & Stedman, Pub., 1848) Children's morality tale about barter-trade at a general store/author's collection

The Poultry Book, by John C. Bennett, M. D., (Boston: Phillips, Sampson & Co., 1850)

The World As You Dream It, by John Perkins, (Rochester, VT: Destiny Books, 1994) Source of Giving Back to Earth Concept

The World Book Encyclopedia, by Field Enterprises Educational Corp., (Chicago: Field Enterprises Ed. Corp., 1968, vol. 15) p. 636 Potash defined AND (1968, vol. 17) p. 810 Geographic information on the Susquehanna River

"Wall Stenciling." AMERICANA, by Wendy Murphy, (New York, N Y: The American Heritage Society, May 1973, vol. 1, No. 2) Source of "Fancy Painting" reference

Author's Note:

The creation of *The Farmers' Museum and Historic Village, Cooperstown, New York,* was a labor of love. Begun in the summer of 2000, it was completed in the spring of 2004. One of the most important and valuable aspects of this book is the incorporation of suggestions made to me by a multitude of advisors. I wish to acknowledge these contributions and offer my deepest gratitude for this wide-ranging assistance. I would like to note a special debt of gratitude to consultant Hugh MacDougall, Cooperstown Village Historian, for sharing his vast knowledge and offering wise insights.

When I first began work on this book, I never dreamed that it would take nearly four years to complete. Nor did I imagine the remarkable journey on which I was about to embark. I came to view the process of historical research as a vibrant and exciting treasure hunt for the truth about the way real people, from real places, lived their lives in the past. I have been greatly changed by this experience and hope that, for young explorers, this book will both inform them and spark a desire to join in this fascinating quest.

Rebecca D.M. Todd – April 10, 2004, Unadilla, NY